ROBIN
LORD CORBETT
OF CASTLE VALE

ROBIN
LORD CORBETT
OF CASTLE VALE

22 December 1933 – 19 February 2012

A LIFE WELL LIVED

by Val Corbett

First published in 2013 on behalf of the author by
Scotforth Books (www.scotforthbooks.com)
ISBN   978-1-904244-90-5
Typesetting and design by Carnegie Publishing, Lancaster.
Printed in the UK by Jellyfish Solutions

Contents

Robin Corbett: Career 1

Obituary from *Daily Telegraph* 4

The Beginning in Oz 6

National Service 9

Robin's 5-Year Plan 11

Why I wanted to be an MP (in Robin's own words) 13

The 1974 Election 14

Losing ... 22

... And Winning 23

Giving up the Commons 23

Third Bite of the Cherry 24

On the Red Benches ... 25

Nelson Mandela 28

My Words at the Funeral 31

Tributes 33

Memorial in the Robing Room of the House of Lords 38

More Tributes 41

What people said about Robin 52

One of his legacies ... 70

Robin Corbett: Career

Elected MP for Hemel Hempstead, 1974–79

His Private Members' Bill in 1976 won the right to anonymity for rape victims – and defendants in rape cases unless convicted. (Thatcher government revoked the defendants' right to anonymity.)

Elected MP for Birmingham Erdington, 1983–2001

Chairman of House of Commons Home Affairs Select Committee, 1999–2001.

Labour front-bench spokesman on broadcasting and media (led for Labour in Broadcasting Bill, 1989–90) from 1987–94 and disabled people's rights from 1994–95.

Appointed to House of Lords, June 2001, as a working peer

Elected Chair of Labour Peers, 2005–2011

Interests included sustainable development, renewable energy, the media, architecture and athletics.

CAMPAIGNS : chairman, British Committee for Iran Freedom; chairman, All-Party Parliamentary Penal Affairs Group; vice chairman, Indo-British Parliamentary Group; chairman, Friends of Cyprus; vice chairman, All-Party Motor Group; member of sustainable development and renewable energy group; foremost in dirty blood campaign. Former member, Wilton Park Academic Council; vice president, Lotteries Council; treasurer, ANZAC group, All-Party Multiple Sclerosis group and the Farm Animal Welfare co-ordinating executive; secretary of Labour's Civil Liberties group; council member of the Royal College of Veterinary Surgeons, Save the Children, Rehab UK; sponsor of the Terrence Higgins Trust; and a patron of the Forum on Prisoner Education and the National Association of Ex-Offenders.

Lord Corbett took his title from a part of his former constituency, which in World War Two was a Spitfire airfield and then later a tower block estate, whose residents have rebuilt their lives through a Housing Action Trust – now a Neighbourhood Partnership Board of which he was chairman. Some 30 tower blocks have been demolished, replaced with double-storey houses and bungalows. Mortality rates in Castle Vale have been reduced, crime has been cut to the lowest in the City of Birmingham and educational standards have improved. In this former sink estate there is now a waiting list for homes and schools.

Opposite: Robin in House of Lords robes, July 2001.

3

Obituary from *Daily Telegraph*

LORD CORBETT OF Castle Vale was a journalist who for 23 years as a Labour MP, and 10 more as a peer, campaigned for civil liberties, animal welfare and a free press. Robin Corbett won for rape victims – and defendants in rape cases unless convicted – the right to anonymity, piloting through a Private Members' Bill in 1976. When *The Sun*, after the 1986 Ealing vicarage rape case, found a way round the prohibition, Corbett denounced it as a 'sewer'. He protested when, in 1988, Margaret Thatcher's government abolished anonymity for rape defendants.

Corbett's campaigning for greater transparency in government also bore fruit, though he criticised New Labour's Freedom of Information Act as 'watered-down'. Believing that Britain had a 'national passion for secrecy', he backed Clement Freud's Bill which was on the way through when James Callaghan's government fell in 1979 and later promoted a similar Bill of his own; he also sent a frisson through Whitehall by naming the head of MI5.

Ironically Corbett in 1975 had to apologise to the Commons after helping a journalist install a bugging device in the office of a fellow Labour MP – who was not in the know – to show how easily it could be done. Ahead of his time quite obviously.

Chairing the All-Party Penal Affairs Group, he campaigned for penal reform and pressed unsuccessfully for repeal of the Prevention of Terrorism Act. His efforts to secure a ban on dangerous dogs – and his campaigning for a ban on hunting with hounds – met with greater success.

He defended the BBC trenchantly and saw the Thatcher government's plans to award ITV franchises to the highest bidder as proof that 'the vandals have won'. As for the tabloids, Corbett said Parliament would be forced to clean up the 'sewer end' of the press unless journalists and proprietors did it themselves. Would the Leveson Committee have been necessary if Corbett had prevailed?

Corbett got into Parliament at the fourth attempt, winning Hemel Hempstead at the October 1974 election by 485 votes from the Conservatives. His stay was short-lived, though he made his mark campaigning for corruption in the Metropolitan Police to be severely punished; in 1979 he lost by 4,989 votes to the future Tory Attorney General Nicholas Lyell.

He hoped to win back his seat and a majority of party branches at Hemel Hempstead nominated Corbett to stand again, but the Left-wing constituency executive left him off the shortlist in favour of Paul Boateng who went on to lose the seat comprehensively in the 1983 general election. At the same election Corbett returned to Westminster – nationally a disaster for Labour – for normally safe Birmingham Erdington, winning by just 231 votes. He made such an impact on the Home Affairs Committee that in 1985 Neil Kinnock made him a front-bench spokesman. John Smith kept him as spokesman on the media and national heritage; Tony Blair made him spokesman on disability, then, in 1995, dropped him from the front bench.

When Labour came to power in 1997, Corbett returned to the Home Affairs Committee, chairing it from 1999. He left the Commons in 2001, taking a life peerage named after an estate in his constituency. He next became chairman of the Castle Vale neighbourhood management board, formed to regenerate the locality, helping to secure £86 million of investment.

He published two books of humorous anecdotes with his wife Val Hudson Corbett, 'Can I Count on Your Support?' (1986) and 'On the Campaign Trail' (1987).

The Beginning in Oz

ONE AFTERNOON IN 1935, a small crowd gathered outside the Western Australian Parliament protesting at the cut in unemployment benefit. It was a peaceful protest until a tall man – and so easily identifiable – threw a stone at the building and broke a window. That man was Tom Corbett and his impetuous action had a life-changing result. Quite against the trend, Tom and his family – including his two-year-old son Robin – were immediately deported to Britain. Years later, Robin was on a parliamentary trip to Western Australian and told the story to the Premier. The following day, proving the Aussie sense of humour, he presented Robin with a bill for the window. If it wasn't for his deportation, Australian politics might have been very different, as Robin would always have been a political animal wherever he lived. Indeed, he started young:

Robin at a debating society at Holly Lodge Grammar School, Smethwick, West Midlands.

*I didn't really like school until about the last year. It had been
a private school but the first year I went there it had come into
the state sector, but of course all the masters were from that
background and I adjusted to this with great difficulty so I kept
getting into trouble and getting generous doses of the cane. Then
somebody had the bright idea of making five or six of us, who
used to get into scrapes, prefects and things changed overnight.*

Robin's parents met on board a ship bound for Perth. They were
instantly attracted to one another but there was a problem: Marguerite's
husband Fred and their three children. That shipboard romance resulted
in her divorcing Fred and swiftly marrying Tom Corbett – something,
she told me, she regretted from day one. When the family had to leave
Australia they settled in West Bromwich, West Midlands, deep in
the Black Country, where Tom sweated in the local foundry. This life
was completely alien to Marguerite, born and brought up in the pretty
Sussex village of Cuckfield.

One evening in the 90's, I saw a photo of Marguerite wheeling the
pram with her twins, Robin and Judy with James walking beside her in
West Bromwich.

    "You look very sad," I commented.
    "Yes," she said, "that's because when we were deported I had to leave
three children behind."
    We were flabbergasted and Robin said, "But you never told me."
And she replied, "But you never asked."
    As Robin said afterwards, "When she arrived I was one of three and
when she left I was one of six!"

Robin eventually met his step brother Peter and family when we
visited Western Australia (he bent down and kissed the airport tarmac
after landing in Perth) but unfortunately was never able to track down
the other two.
Tom Corbett had been in the First World War trenches at 16 having
lied about his age. The experience led to heavy drinking and violence

towards his wife and family. However, I believe this dysfunctional family made Robin stronger and more stubborn. When he decided a cause was just, he was not swayed from the path. A case in point was his firm support for the Iranian Resistance in 1989 which was definitely seen as bad for his career. He continued to support them together with many members of both Houses of Parliament until his death.

Robin's boyhood was not all bleak; to escape from her unhappy marriage, Marguerite Corbett cycled with Robin, his twin sister Judy and their big brother James the length and breadth of England, Scotland, Wales and Ireland – north and south. Robin enjoyed cycling and became a junior champion. When, much later, we used to cycle in Holland (because there were no hills!), everyone thought he would lag behind. In fact, they only caught sight of his flapping shirt tails as he left everyone else way behind. As the family couldn't afford to keep him at school, Robin left at 16 and became a copy boy at the *Birmingham Mail*:

> *My first job after school was as a copy boy on the* Birmingham Mail *having been warned by the careers master at school that the last unfortunate who went into journalism was still making the tea and sweeping the office for a paper called the Smethwick Telephone! After a while I made myself a nuisance saying I wanted to be a trainee reporter and they weren't having that so I took a week off and when I went back, and I can see this bloke now, the deputy editor, he looked straight at me and said: 'Feeling better Corbett?' I thought this is it, I'm for the high jump but he calmly announced they'd decided to make me a trainee reporter. I stayed for three years and then had to do National Service.*

I never knew this before but it is so similar to my way into journalism. Though the magazine in Cape Town knew my aspirations they needed a filing clerk, and when I was about to be fired as I was the worst filing clerk ever, the editor Peter Hjul prevailed and I was upgraded to trainee journalist.

National Service

ROBIN WAS CONSCRIPTED to do two years of national service at a camp in Watchet, a training camp for the RAF Regiment, staffed by national service RAF personnel, on the Bristol Channel in West Somerset. Ray Palmer and Bernard Donovan (Don) shared the RAF load ...

Don   Robin was posted to Watchet for two years from March 1952 and we joined him that August. By then Robin had become firmly established in the orderly room and at first I thought he was in charge of the camp rather than the C.O.!

Ray   My abiding memory of Robin was crouched over the typewriter, mug of tea to hand. It wasn't long before he persuaded someone in authority that we needed a camp magazine and he was allocated time to produce this ... his first taste as editor.

Don   Robin's flair for journalism and organising ability in general were put to good use on that magazine and he spent hours producing copies from an ancient Gestetner machine.

Ray   At the time he considered life in the RAF an unnecessary intrusion on his civilian activities, but in later life we talked of the benefit of national service and often reminisced about our time at Watchet, particularly the Masons Arms – the pub with cider at 10p a pint.

Don   It was great news when we learnt of Robin's election to Parliament and I'd like to think some of his formative years in RAF Watchet helped him achieve that. When he was elevated to the Lords we enjoyed some memorable visits with him. A good friend, we miss him very much.

Ray   I will never forget Robin and consider my life having been enriched by knowing him both during national service and the many years of friendship afterwards.

Back in civvy street, Robin went to London and talked his way into the *Streatham News* as a reporter. He didn't stay there long for he was given a trial on the then mighty *Daily Mirror*. Unfortunately that didn't work out, athough on the day he left – last in, first out – his stories were on both the front and back pages of the paper. He then went to work for an Hungarian news agency.

Hoping to create a happy family, he married at 21 but it was not a happy partnership. Every time they had a problem, his wife insisted on moving home. They moved ten times in 13 years. No wonder, during our marriage, he made it clear that our cottage in Piccotts End in Hertfordshire was where we stayed. We lived there happily for 41 years, and I still do. Incidentally, the way he bought the cottage was very Corbett-like. Canvassing in the 1966 election, the occupants of the cottage told him they were moving. Robin asked to look around and then said, 'I'll buy it from you.' The owners replied, 'You don't have to do that, we're going to vote for you anyway.' Robin's first marriage ended after 13 years and after that he spent much time in the law courts trying to get access to see his children, Susannah and Adam. Tragically his third child, 18-month-old Lucy, died in an accident and he told me he thought about her every single day of his life. It was why he was able to write such a moving letter to Gordon and Sarah Brown after their baby died. Meanwhile, in Cape Town, South Africa, with pretty much the same family life and violent father, I did three jobs in order to raise the fare to get to the newspaper Mecca that was Fleet Street. After a few false starts,I managed to get there and work on a precariously financed, independent women's magazine. When the magazine inevitably folded, it was relatively easy to get another job at a trade magazine called *Furnishing World*, with offices opposite the Old Vic in Waterloo. After the Hungarian News Agency, Robin landed a job as a reporter on the same magazine.

His version of our meeting: He was walking along Fleet Street when he glanced down and saw some little fingers. A good-hearted chap, he leaned down and hauled me up out of the gutter.

What really happened: I was wearing a new dress and was unsure about it. As I passed through a swing door to go to lunch, I asked a woman colleague, 'Does this dress make me look dumpy?' A voice to my right said, 'Yes it does.' I looked up … and up … and saw the first sight of my life's companion. (He called me Dumpy for ages afterwards.) When we first got together, over dinner one evening, we compiled his life plan.

Number one on that plan was easy …

Robin's 5-Year Plan

1. Happily married to you
2. MP
3. Government job
4. Demanding executive job with IPC
5. Play it happily pear-shaped

Witnessed by X (Val, her mark)

Miraculously, it all came to pass!

Robin didn't stay long at the magazine. He left to become a reporter on *Farmers Weekly* and after a few years was promoted to an influential political editor, then deputy editor, before moving to IPC magazines in charge of training their journalists (see number 4 above).

In his spare time he concentrated on travelling the long road to the green benches of the House of Commons.

Our wedding day, 22 May 1970, the Guildhall, City of London.

Why I wanted to be an MP (in Robin's own words)

"My parents were both political and while my friends were kicking a football around, some of my earliest memories involve standing on street corners handing out leaflets with my twin sister and elder brother. My first political campaign was to picket, with my siblings, for more pocket money. We marched round and round the back yard carrying placards calling for 6*d* a week more pocket money. And we got it – eventually.

My siblings did not go into politics but I had the strong feeling that I wanted to help change the world and you need this attitude because there are days when you wonder why the hell you wanted to do it!

As Fred Daley an Australian politician once said: 'Politics is a funny game. One day you're a rooster and the next you're a feather duster."

The 1974 Election

THERE WERE TWO elections in 1974. Robin's slogan for the one in February was 'Call for Corbett'. He lost by 187 votes, so in the October election, the slogan changed to: 'Call for Corbett ... LOUDER.' Luckily, they did, and he scraped in with 485 votes.

One story of that election: canvassing one day Robin passed a house covered in Liberal posters. Then a man rushed out of that house and called him back.

'Don't worry,' he said, 'I'm going to vote for you.'

'Then why all those Liberal posters?'

'Oh that's because I don't want the neighbours to know how I vote.'

Photo chosen for his election leaflet. (Some young women pasted it in their windows but facing INTO their room!)

Mmmmmm!

"Do you think they saw us?"

Above: The Corbetts: tea and political empathy - a series of photos for a magazine article (these two were not used)

Canvassing in February – we were both exhausted and soon after Robin broke his elbow and was in pain and plaster. He still lost!

Polly's good luck card: at least she got the colours right

'It took me four tries before I finally made it. In October 1974 I was elected in Hemel Hempstead, Hertfordshire, with a magnificent majority of 485.

Euphoric with a (very) long-awaited victory

Elizabeth the Second by the Grace of God of the United Kingdom of Great Britain and Northern Ireland and of Our other Realms and Territories Queen Head of the Commonwealth Defender of the Faith To Our right trusty and well beloved Robin Corbett of Erdington in Our County of West Midlands Chevalier Greeting **Whereas** Our Parliament for arduous and urgent affairs concerning Us the state and defence of Our United Kingdom and the Church is now met at Our City of Westminster We strictly enjoining command you upon the faith and allegiance by which you are bound to Us that considering the difficulty of the said affairs and dangers impending (waiving all excuses) you be personally present at Our aforesaid Parliament with Us and with the Prelates Nobles and Peers of Our said Kingdom to treat and give your counsel upon the affairs aforesaid And this as you regard Us and Our honour and the safety and defence of the said Kingdom and Church and dispatch of the said affairs in nowise do you omit **Witness** Ourself at Westminster in the afternoon of the fifth day of July in the fiftieth year of Our Reign

PHILLIPS

To ROBIN LORD CORBETT OF CASTLE VALE

A Writ of Summons to Parliament

PHILLIPS

'I came into the Commons in 1974 and I loved the place when I arrived, even the pink tapes hanging from pegs in the members' cloakroom. They were there to hang your sword before entering the Chamber. That should have warned me because one of the first things that happened was I got shouted at by the speaker, Selwyn Lloyd – it's the things people don't explain to you, you see. I was speaking in the Chamber one day and I'd drawn my usual crowd, you know, about three, and I was talking to the speaker. Then all of a sudden Selwyn gets up and shouts, "Order! Order!" and I thought, my God, I'm going to get six months. He barked at me, "Will the honourable member stop staring at me!"

'The trouble is, when you do finally get elected to the House of Commons, there's no certificate or illuminated address. At least when you become a lord, you get sent a Writ of Summons.

'As a new MP, you just turn up at the Commons and the policeman on the gate ticks your name against the *Daily Telegraph* election supplement. So if they leave your name out by mistake, you don't get in!

'After my first day in the House I told my wife, "The walls reek of history. I am not fit to walk on the floors." By the end of the week I said, "Blimey, there are an awful lot of stupid people in there, how did THEY get in?"'

Robin threw himself into constituency work during his first parliamentary years, doing around 75–80 hours a week. It was a minority Labour government with so many all-night sittings that he was seldom at home. One morning I was driving to work in Fleet Street when he was coming home from the House and we worked out we must have passed each other on the M1. In fact he suggested I show our young daughter Polly his photo and tell her he would see her when she was 21! But he saw much more of her way before that time, because, though he halved the local swing to the Tories in 1979, he still came second – and the mountain of whitebait served while waiting to go to the count has meant I can never again eat this fish.

Robin expected to be selected to fight the Hemel Hempstead seat again and he got nominations from most of the constituency branches. Unfortunately, the Militant Tendency moved in and through some pretty shabby work, Paul Boateng was chosen as the Labour parliamentary candidate.

Julius Silverman, the retiring MP gave solid support to his successor with wife and young Polly

It was a bitter blow and I remember him saying to me, 'That's my political career, over.'

Ah, but fate took a hand. When the 1983 election was called he was working (unhappily) in a public relations consultancy when Birmingham Erdington's MP (since 1945!) stepped down and Robin applied and went on the selection panel. It was about three weeks before that election. He won the selection and became their parliamentary Labour candidate.

During the election a full busload of Hemel party activists went to canvass for Robin in Erdington, spreading the word at how assiduous an MP he was and how lucky they were to have him. These Hemel lot must have done well as Robin was elected, though with the slimmest of margins.

And the result in Hemel? The Labour candidate came third. If Robin had been standing, he would have come second as it was a rotten year for Labour. By going elsewhere his political career, far from over, was regenerated.

From an article in the *House Magazine 1998*

'It's a funny way to earn a living: if ever I write about my time in this place that's what I shall call it. What other job gets you involved in things – and at such hours – that others would find eccentric?

'Home late the other night to find a message from a former constituent who feels every effort should be made to recognise Albania. Then there was the constituent who rang me near to midnight to complain about a BBC programme. When I asked why he didn't ring them he said their phone was always engaged.

'There are two parts to an MP's job, Westminster and the work in the constituency. I always preferred the work in the constituency because it kept your feet on the ground and reminded you that you're doing this job for other people, not yourself.

'I actually enjoy 'surgeries' though the misery factor has risen greatly. But we all have constituents with more problems than we've got answers. I have two of them. One is kind enough to collect up problems every time he sets foot outside his house, even knocking doors asking for them. The other simply sits and thinks about them … they come faster than I can cope and each time I get an answer he bowls me another. Mind, he won't know what's hit him because I have unleashed every voluntary and statutory organisation on his case. On second thoughts I know he will recover and return.

'Strange things happen to MPs. A colleague remembers doing a talk to sixth formers and at tea afterwards he said to one attractive pupil, "What are you going to do when you leave school?"

'To which she replied, "I was thinking of going home. What did you have in mind?"

'During the October '74 general election, I called on a woman who said she was not going to vote for me because she hadn't got her supply of bin bags – I went to the nearby council depot and collected some for her. As I won that seat by 485 I have to ask myself if I hadn't got her the bin bags, would my majority have been one less?'

***

Losing …

'When I lost the seat in 1979, it was a horrible feeling. You feel hurt, it's all your fault and it's worse in a sense when you live locally, as we did. I'd had a book in me for some time so to try to cope with this dreadful situation I wrote 20,000 on my old sit-up-and-beg typewriter in about two days, and this had a very bad effect on my wrists. I went to the doctor and he bound them up and I went off walking around the town. Within minutes Val got a phone call saying, 'I've just heard the most terrible news that Robin's slashed his wrists' – it had never crossed my mind!

'But Hemel Hempstead was a safe seat compared with my majority in 1983, in Birmingham Erdington, of 221, after five gut-wrenching recounts. Mind, each time they did a recount I got a couple more votes so I asked them to keep going!'

… And Winning

In 1983, as MP for Birmingham, Erdington – back to his West Midlands roots – with another wafer-slim majority he once again worked his socks off for 18 years, particularly with the-then sink estate, Castle Vale.

Celebration with banners and neighbours after winning Erdington

With many others, Robin was one of the moving spirits to transform the area into the internationally acknowledged regeneration model it is now. So impressed with the input from residents was he that he took the name of this estate as his title and served as chair to the Castle Vale Neighbourhood Partnership Board until his death.

'When I left in 2001 I had a majority of over 12,000 so I suppose I must have done something right.'

Giving up the Commons

With Birmingham Erdington now a safe Labour seat, there had been speculation in newspapers that he would give up but he had assured everyone that he would stand again in 2001, which he had every intention of doing.

However, a few weeks before the general election, Robin had an unfortunate encounter with a difficult and abusive constituent at his regular advice surgery. When he came home he said, 'I think I am going to change my mind and not stand for re-election. I was rude to a constituent for the first time and I think I need to hand over to a younger MP.' Though I tried to persuade him that his knowledge and compassion made him an ideal MP, he was adamant. 'This is *really* the end of my political career,' he told me – again. Oh yes?

23

A special look at the career of Erdington MP Robin Corbett

Corbett: A credit to the community

Caption: Corbett: a credit to the community

Third Bite of the Cherry

Having turned down a peerage in 1997 because the powers that be wanted to parachute their own candidate into the seat ('Only the Erdington Labour Party has the right to choose their candidate,' he told them), that door was firmly closed as 'they' never offer honours twice. So we sat down to make a list of 'Things I Could Do When No Longer An MP' – a short list with working for a charity or voluntary organisation being his favourite option.

Imagine our astonishment when Robin was sounded out for a

peerage and asked whether he would accept. Of course he would, and did! We might have thought it was a dream but then Robin received this letter from 10 Downing Street (overleaf).

Another revival of his political career! He joined an influx of long-serving MPs who knew how the Palace of Westminster worked. This, when mixed with the removal of 90% of hereditary peers, made the Upper House far more aware of the world outside the Westminster bubble.

The worst part of this great moment was keeping it secret from our family and friends who were bemoaning that all his knowledge and experience would be wasted. I had to bite my tongue many times; it was a long six weeks. The day before the announcement we invited Polly to lunch in a hotel in London, something we had never done before. She arrived looking apprehensive.

'Which one of you is dying?' she asked before saying hello.

When we replied neither, she said, 'Please don't tell me you're getting divorced.'

Then she saw the waiter bringing the champagne to our table and relaxed.

On the Red Benches ...

ROBIN THRIVED IN the House of Lords. He appreciated the lack of confrontation and the more erudite debates. At first he was awed with the sheer expertise of some members – the Law Lords, several former influential Cabinet members and so on – but like most of the former MPs in the place he very quickly decided if he let that stop him, he would never make a speech.

While waiting to make his maiden speech, he listened as one of the Tories opposite said: "When I was 65, thirty years ago ..." ('I hope I can make as good a speech when I am his age,' he told me.)

Of course, like his colleagues he railed against some of the more archaic traditions – like any break in proceedings being described as 'House Adjourned During Pleasure' (conjuring up some comic imagery!). And while the Commons voted in the 'No' or 'Yea' lobby,

1O DOWNING STREET
LONDON SW1A 2AA

From the Secretary for Appointments

W E Chapman

25 May 2001

Dear Mr. Corbett,

The Prime Minister has asked me to let you know that he has recommended to The Queen that a Barony of the United Kingdom for Life be conferred upon you.

Should The Queen approve this recommendation, your Life Peerage will be announced on Saturday 2 June, in a supplement to the London Gazette; details of the list of names will be released to the press on Friday 1 June, under embargo until midnight. This information is, of course, confidential until published on 2 June.

Your title will be settled on a recommendation from Garter King of Arms, who will get in touch with you direct in due course.

Yours sincerely,

William Chapman.

WILLIAM CHAPMAN

Robin Corbett Esq

the lords called theirs 'Content' and 'Not Content'.

But he was as active there as he had been in the 'Other Place', as parliamentarians call it. His energy, humour and ability to hear all sides of an argument culminated in a unanimous vote in 2005 to elect him chair of the Labour peers, and he was subsequently re-elected until his death.

Extract from a talk he gave on life in the Lords

'This century has thrown up three categories of political leaders. *The good*, which includes Winston Churchill and Franklyn Roosevelt; *the bad*, which is Hitler and Stalin; and the third is *the special*, the person who transcends politics. I can think of only three in the last century who fall into this class – Mahatma Gandhi, the Dalai Lama and Nelson Mandela. And because of my job I have met two of the three, within two weeks.

'The problem when you meet them is what do you do? You can't simply say, "How are you?" or ask for their autograph.

'I thought both of them were very similar – not so much saintly but at ease with themselves, with a quiet dignity on top of rock-solid belief in their cause. I'd call them natural leaders.

'The Dalai Lama simply shook my hand, acknowledged my interest in his homeland of Tibet and looked at me inviting a question.

'There was only one I could ask: "When do you think you'll be able to go home?"

'He smiled and said, "I am always hopeful that China will want this to happen and we do keep talking." He said it was important that, just as China had waited 100 years to return to Hong Kong to what it sees as its family, so he thought it would eventually be with both Tibet and Taiwan. I applaud his optimism but must say I don't share it.'

Nelson Mandela

'MY WIFE WAS born in Cape Town and asked me to join her annual trip back home. I always said I wouldn't step on to South African soil until and unless Nelson Mandela was free, and not only free, but president. I thought it would be another 20 years but it happened 8 months later.' (On this visit I took Robin to see my first editor, Peter Hjul, who had been under house arrest, but with pressure from the National Union of Journalists and others, was released to leave the country. He showed us the NUJ petition – and the second name on that list was Robin Corbett.)

'On my first visit we went and saw Mandela's tiny cell in Robben Island and were taken to the quarry where prisoners hacked rocks in baking sun. On his first visit there when president, Mr Mandela picked up a stone and placed it on the ground. One by one, his fellow ex-prisoners picked their own stones and placed them on top of his. This pyre stands today and guides (all former prisoners) are always asked which stone is Mr Mandela's. Answer: "The one right at the bottom."

'We were told that one of the few perks in that prison was football matches. When I asked how they managed for away games, the guide couldn't stop laughing.

'Both Houses welcomed President Mandela in 1996 with a spectacular ceremony in Westminster Hall – a triumphant occasion complete with trumpeters and the full pomp and ceremony for which we are rightfully known. Speaker Baroness Betty Boothroyd told me later that at a state dinner at Buckingham Palace the night before, she had told the president about the many stone steps leading into Westminster Hall. At the time there were no handrails and he was a frail 78 years old. But when she met him just before the ceremony he told her he had done a recce at 6 a.m. that morning! Though she had to support him as his legs and eyesight were not too good (his eyes were damaged by the bright sunlight while breaking rocks in the Robben Island quarry), they managed well enough.

'Despite his physical frailty, he was mesmerising when he spoke and he captured the full attention of everyone in that historic hall. He spoke without resentment about the denial of democracy to the majority of the population for 85 years and illustrated his greatness by adding: "we return to this honoured place neither with pikes, nor with a desire for revenge, nor even a plea to your distinguished selves to assuage our hunger for bread. We come to you as friends."

'My wife and I were just behind Jeremy Thorpe, former leader of the Liberals, one of the first British party leaders to support the Anti-Apartheid Movement. Mr Mandela, on his way out of the building, made a point of shaking his hand.

'When we heard President Obama speak in that same hall, Val and I thought he displayed that same quiet authority and powerful presence of the Dalai Lama and Nelson Mandela.'

***

At the 30th anniversary of gaining entry into the Palace of Westminster, Robin celebrated with fellow parliamentarians who had arrived at the Commons with him, including Bruce Grocott and Ann Taylor, with a special dinner. The cake was decorated with symbols representing all the prime ministers in office during these years: pipe (Harold Wilson); anchor (James Callaghan); handbag (Margaret Thatcher); cricket bat (John Major); and guitar (Tony Blair).

Robin's Funeral

WE CHOSE ROBIN'S favourite music for the ceremony and it all fitted in magnificently. The organist played Elgar's Nimrod as Robin's coffin entered the ancient St Mary's Church and reached its crescendo as his coffin was placed on the plinth. A beauteous red rose from his twin sister Judy in Australia was its only adornment. The hymns were I Vow to Thee My Country and of course Jerusalem. Later, Lark Ascending by Vaughan Williams gave time and space to remember him. And of course The Red Flag as we followed the coffin out of the church and to the crematorium.

Afterwards champagne and some delicious finger food at The Marchmont Arms, down the road from the church and within walking distance of our house. A friend summed it up: "A wake yesterday in the best Irish tradition. We mourned but we laughed as we remembered a great man (though not a saint!)"

My Words at the Funeral

ROBIN AND I had a marriage based on a shared sense of humour. We made each other laugh over the 45 years we had together but he wasn't a saint, as I've had to point out to other people – including himself – from time to time. Once, I came into the kitchen and he was having a fight with a paper bag – and the bag won. But the biggest argument we ever had was over the Miliband brothers – both of whom have sent lovely messages.

I was very supportive of his political life because I once met a rather embittered wife in the family room of the House of Commons, and she said: 'Keep up with what he's doing otherwise you will be locked out of the main obsession in his life.' I know what she meant. Once I looked up to find him staring at me with a particularly loving expression. When I asked him softly what he was thinking about, he said: 'The Housing Finance Act.'

During the 22 years he spent in the House of Commons we often went canvassing, which provided a fund of stories for our book, *Can I Count on Your Support?* Once he was speaking to a potential voter when his agent dragged him away. When Robin asked him why, as he was about to persuade the man to vote Labour, his agent replied: 'You couldn't see what I saw. While he was speaking to you, his dog was eating his dinner.'

Robin was a very hands-on MP and peer. He liked speaking to constituents, a fact so many have mentioned in their letters and cards. And the spread of the people he helped was surprisingly wide, from MPs and peers who thanked him for mentoring them when they first entered the House to a taxi driver in Birmingham – and a young man who reminded me that Robin had contacted him when his bicycle was stolen (it was in the local paper). Robin suggested that he did some odd jobs around our house so he could buy another bike. I know that wherever I went I met people who said, 'Your husband helped me.' It was what he did. And he enjoyed doing it.

But most of you don't know that Robin was brought up in a really dysfunctional family with parents who hardly spoke to each other, often communicating through their three children. His father, a foundry worker, had been in the war trenches at 16 having lied about his age and he was not only violent to his wife but also to Robin whom for some reason he appeared to hate. It was one of the many things that linked us, as my background was pretty much the same. And yet this upbringing was the spur which made Robin strong enough to reach the heights of political life and want to help hundreds of people.

Many years later he read *Birdsong* by Sebastian Faulkes and said he understood far more about why his father had returned from war so damaged. It's what I admired so much about him – he liked to delve into what made people tick. And he always saw the best in them. Despite his busy political life, and definitely because of his background, he valued family life enormously and enjoyed spending time with his children and grandchildren.

But never did I admire him more than when he was fighting this dreadful disease. Never once, I promise you, did he complain; never once did he say, 'Why me?' Never once did he say, 'It's not fair.' He accepted what happened, dealt with it and had what he most wanted, an honourable and dignified decent death in his own home.

I would be letting him down if I collapsed in a heap. But oh, I shall miss him so much – hearing him sing 'The Wild Colonial Boy' after several glasses of wine, and his funny little ways: if you hug, you have to pat at the same time; always bash the corners of a piece of toast before spreading butter; and above all, never trust the driver in front of you if they're wearing a hat.

Robin was a good and faithful servant to his country, to his constituents, to the Labour Party, to Parliament and to his family. Today I pay tribute to the work he did and celebrate a life that was worth living.

Tributes

Bruce Grocott

Robin and I have been friends through all the ups and downs of political life for almost 40 years. Val and my wife Sally have likewise been friends, united amongst other things by that toughest of challenges – being married to politicians. Sally summed it up when Robin died: 'Life,' she said, 'won't be so much fun.'

Robin was a wonderful friend. He was an outstanding, hands-on, constituency MP for Hemel Hempstead, then Birmingham Erdington; a politician of great skill in both the Commons and the Lords. He was a man rich in his interests and in the love of his family. By any standards he was a big personality. You knew when Robin was in the room.

And his humour never left him. Just a few weeks before he died I was visiting him in hospital when the nurse came round with the menu for the evening meal. Robin made his choice then looked up at the nurse and said, 'now can I see the wine list please?'

Robin was born in Western Australia. He was there for just two years when his father, an active trade unionist, was deported and the family returned to England. During a demonstration his father had thrown a brick through a window of the Western Australian Parliament which meant deportation and the family settled in West Bromwich. On leaving school and completing national service, Robin started his career as a journalist but politics beckoned.

His road to the House of Commons wasn't easy. He fought Hemel Hempstead in 1966 and lost. He was then persuaded by the party – Robin could never say no – to fight a by-election in West Derbyshire in November 1967. It was freezing and Robin swears that at one village meeting the only people in the hall were himself, the party chairman and one man at the back who Robin later discovered was the caretaker. Needless to say Robin lost that election as well. He fought Hemel again in February 1974 and lost by an agonising 187 votes. Then: triumph. He won in October 1974, with a cliff edge majority of 485. I won as well for the first time after previous defeats. Robin took great delight in the fact that my majority of just 331 was even smaller than his. And the Labour government's overall majority was just three. Robin and I would joke that whenever Harold Wilson saw us together in the Commons, he would say, 'for heaven's sake lads when you go home tonight drive carefully'.

Robin's great achievement in that first Parliament was the Private Members' Bill he sponsored, rightly described by *The Times* as ground-breaking, which provided for anonymity for victims of rape. He pretty well achieved the impossible – you are not supposed to be able to get difficult and controversial bills through Parliament as a backbencher. But Robin brought all his skills to bear – tenacity, courage, persuasion and conviction – and the bill became law.

But there is no justice in politics. After the Winter of Discontent Labour lost the 1979 general election. Robin lost his seat and I, of course, came out in sympathy.

But in 1983 Robin bounced back as the member for Birmingham Erdington, again with a cliff-hanging majority, this time just 231. But at last he had found a political berth which would see him through with increased majorities until he retired from the Commons 18 years later in 2001.

Robin was appointed successively by Neil Kinnock, John Smith and Tony Blair to a series of important jobs including handling Labour's policy on the media. If only more people in power had listened then to Robin Corbett with his passionate criticism of lax media standards, and his denunciation of the way in which media power was allowed to be concentrated in the hands of a small number of men, there would be no need for a Leveson Inquiry now.

In truth, Robin symbolised Labour's lost generation. Eighteen years in opposition was precisely the time when Robin's political talents were at their peak. Had Labour been in power during those years, he would undoubtedly have held high ministerial office.

With Labour back in power in 1997, Robin was then in his sixties, but he was never one to sit back. He became chairman of the Home Affairs Select Committee. Here was a man, the architect of the

Sexual Offences Bill, former Home Affairs front-bench spokesman, champion of civil liberties, with a coveted senior role which he relished.

Robin had many interests outside Parliament. He would often ring me on a Saturday night about the football results. Needless to say, the member for Birmingham Erdington was a strong supporter of Aston Villa. But nobody's perfect.

In 2001 Robin was made a Life Peer. The title he chose was Lord Corbett of Castle Vale. Castle Vale, built in the 1960s and part of his former constituency, over 20 blocks of high-storey flats. Robin became chairman of the Management Board. His leadership and energy brought new business investment into the community, including a modern shopping centre.

In 2005 Robin was elected unopposed as chairman of the 239-strong Labour group in the House of Lords. He was a natural for the job – popular and effective.

By any standards, Robin's public life was hugely successful. But it is Robin the man who we remember most. His warmth, his humour, his loyalty, his deep concern for others, his generosity. In all the years I knew him I can hardly recall him ever speaking ill of anyone. There was no malice in him. And this warmth was reciprocated. If Robin had any enemies in politics, I had never met one.

It has become fashionable these days to say that all politicians are in it for themselves or can't be trusted. No one who had ever met Robin Corbett would ever say that again.

We shall all miss him enormously. But the loss above all is that of his wife Val. They say humour is at the heart of a successful marriage and they had it in abundance. And we all share the loss felt by Robin's children, Susannah, Adam and Polly, and all the other members of his family.

Robin lived life to the full, still working hard just a few weeks before he died. He enriched the lives of those who knew him and improved the lives of so many who came to him for help. In 78 years you can't do much better than that.

Iranian Resistance

Two days after his funeral, the Iranian Resistance organised a magnificent ceremony of remembrance at their Paris HQ. Dignitaries had come from all over Europe to pay their tributes and my family and I – his daughters Susannah and Polly, sister-in-law Mary and granddaughter Maya – were moved by the love and appreciation they expressed for the chairman of their parliamentary All-Party group in trying to free Iran. As part of the ceremony, I released a dove of peace which circled the shrine and then went to perch on the huge photograph of Robin.

Releasing the white dove which circled above them then settled on top of Robin's photograph and remained there.

The main shrine to Robin – the family were given large bunches of beautiful white roses which covered the steps.

With Maryam Rajavi, president of the Iranian Resistance who worked closely with Robin over many years.

Castle Vale

Castle Vale organised its own memorial which was well attended, where we heard residents speak about 'our Robin'. One man recalled a problem he'd had with his daughter's education which Robin helped solve. She was then accepted by Cambridge and Robin invited them to the House where they expected him to shake hands and say goodbye. In the event he took them on a tour and then out for a celebratory lunch. And when their daughter applied for a job in New York, Robin's reference, must have swung things for she got this much-coveted position.

Memorial in the Robing Room of the House of Lords

The memorial in the Robing Room of the House of Lords in July 2012 was crowded with peers, MPs, friends and supporters. When I spoke I pointed out how appropriate the room was, because the word 'Robing' is 'Robin' with a 'g' at the end!

Lord Corbett of Castle Vale
22 December 1933 – 19 February 2012

The Robing Room, House of Lords,
26 June 2012

© Universal Pictorial Press & Agency Ltd. London

Robin Corbett fought for justice, democracy, freedom and human rights
throughout his parliamentary career. He was passionate and determined
about all the causes he championed during his 34 years in both Houses,
from prison reform and developing communities to safeguarding civil
liberties. His Private Member's Bill, which ensured the anonymity of
rape victims, augments an impressive body of work. Principled but never
pious, his warmth, humour and easy manner defused many challenging
situations. Robin cared about people and helped many, without fuss or
fanfare, making a real difference to their lives. He will be much missed.

PROGRAMME

Welcome
Baroness Royall of Blaisdon, Leader of the Labour Lords

Introductions to speakers:
Lord Griffiths of Burry Port

RAF Robin
Ray Palmer and Bernard Donovan share memories of their time in Somerset during National Service.

Corbett in the Commons
Finbar McDonnell recalls Robin's assiduousness as MP for the Hemel Hempstead constituency.

Second bite of the cherry
Lord Rooker, a former Birmingham MP, talks about the neighbouring constituency MP in Erdington.

Building a community
Richard Temple-Cox CBE and Angus Kennedy OBE remember Robin's contribution to the regeneration of Castle Vale.

A political life
Lord Grocott discusses Robin's work from Commons backbencher to Chair of the Labour Peers.

Spouse in the House
Lady Corbett reflects on Robin's legacy.

More Tributes

Birmingham Erdington Labour Party organised the first of the annual Robin Corbett lectures at which Tony Robinson held the 100-strong audience in the palm of his hand. A man came up to me afterwards and said he had told Robin, when meeting him in the street, that he had been accepted by Ruskin College, Oxford, but that his company would not release him. 'Leave it to me,' said Robin. A week later, the man received a letter from his firm giving him the time off and informing him that they would even pay all his expenses.

Finally, the local Co-operative funeral home named its new chapel of rest after the first deceased person to enter it, so I cut the ribbon on the 'Lord Corbett Chapel', and afterwards the Mayor of Hemel Hempstead, Polly, and I, released doves outside. They flew over our heads in a kind of salute before making their way home – I hope!

Campaigns

Friends of Cyprus (1974–2012)

From Mary Southcott, Friends of Cyprus Co-ordinator 1987–91, 1997–present

Robin became active in FOC in 1974 at the behest of a constituent whose husband was in Cyprus when the island was divided. He became vice president in 1987 and worked with others to pioneer the meetings of Greek and Turkish Cypriots, first in London and then in January 1989 at the Ledra Palace Hotel in the buffer zone in Nicosia, Cyprus, drafting the communiqué with one of his collection of pens. Fact-finding visits to the island demonstrated his journalistic skills – asking the right questions, discovering what people were thinking, both agreement and disagreement, within and across the two communities. As chair, he led the 1998 delegation to the Maronite villages in the north, meeting the Turkish Cypriot Cyprus EU Association, and then back to the Cyprus Presidential Palace.

He loved showing Cypriot Chevening Scholars around the Palace of Westminster or organising tea or lunch for Cypriot MPs and councillors of the fenced-off city of Famagusta. His last Friends of Cyprus function as president involved meeting the Cyprus Community Media Centre last year, showing excitement at young Cypriots working together. His kindness will be remembered by many Cypriots whom he met and more importantly, listened to.

Personally I will always remember the posted notes and newspaper clippings he sent me, his phone calls and the fact that he got the MS Society to send material to my daughter after he heard she had been diagnosed with the condition. He also spoke to her on the telephone, told her about Freshwinds in Birmingham and was generally one of the politicians who was human to her when she answered my telephone when I was not there.

And, of course, his oft-repeated favourite phrase, which he would like to have been a prophecy, looked forward to the day 'when the next word to follow Cyprus isn't "problem"'.

From Costa Carras, founder member, Friends of Cyprus

His memory will remain evergreen to those of us who worked with him closely over the years. Robin combined in a most wonderful way that 'groundedness' in English life, both the lives of ordinary people and that of the political world, with a broad and deep human sympathy. That human sympathy was what alerted him to the problems of Cyprus and gave him the strength to continue his work for so many years. It has been both a privilege and a pleasure to have worked with Robin for about two decades on an issue which was, and remains, delicate and difficult, but where Robin's particular virtues and above all his good judgement and his humanity, shone so effectively.

From Haris Sophoclides, president, World Federation of Overseas Cypriots

We Cypriots have received the news of Robin's demise with great sadness. A lot of us had worked with him on the Cyprus issue through his association with the Friends of Cyprus as vice chairman and then as chairman since the death of Nicholas Bethel.

Personally, I knew him well and liked his friendly nature and vigorous exchange of jokes and leg-pulls, but his dedication to his beliefs and principles did not suffer or deviate in the least! We shall all miss him and pray for his soul.

Chair Parlimentary all-party Penal Reform Group

From Geoff Dobson OBE, clerk to the group

I first met Robin in 2002 having spent some months talking to MPs and peers about who might best resurrect the All-Party Parliamentary Penal Affairs Group. The group, founded in 1981, had helped to ensure there was a cohort of active and informed parliamentarians keen on reforming our overstretched, and often ineffective, prison system. The group had not met since the 2001 general election and had become officially defunct. Robin's name kept cropping up, from both Houses and from across the political spectrum. As a long-serving MP, with two successful stints at chairing the Home Affairs Select Committee, and now highly respected in the Lords, he emerged as the clear favourite. I nervously and laboriously explained this to Robin, who waited patiently for me to dry up before beaming and exclaiming: 'Don't stop now, you're doing rather well!' He was re-elected at each AGM without challenge for the next decade. The group quickly became one of the best-attended All-Party forums, often holding joint events with other groups to extend the range of those with some appreciation of the need for improvement in this arena of public service. Robin's ease with people from all backgrounds was evident in our meetings and our occasional visits to penal establishments. As we entered a dormitory at the Military Corrective Training Centre in Colchester, detainees leapt from their bunks to salute us. Robin simply smiled and said, 'Now look here, you probably all outrank me from my time in the armed forces, so let's just relax and have a chat.' They could see that he was genuinely interested in what they had to say and ended up telling us a lot more than they had intended. Meetings featured presentations from ministers, officials, those delivering services, former offenders, families of people in custody and have also included serving prisoners.

While extending a relaxed welcome to all, Robin also demonstrated a fierce determination to make prisons more just, humane and effective. The latest report of the work of the prisoner rehabilitation group is dedicated to him and the front cover features his statement: 'A jail sentence shouldn't be about society's revenge, but rather a chance to change the direction of a life.' He would take up the cudgels where he felt an injustice had been done and the testimonies from our meetings prompted numerous questions and debates in the House as well as robust letters to Ministers. Sadly, prison reform does not always win votes and it can be a thankless task for politicians. Robin's unwavering commitment to an unpopular cause marked him out as a leader who inspired others. He was also great fun to work with, an invaluable quality in dealing with a multitude of sorry tales and wasted lives. Robin could always see the potential for change for the better whether in people, in systems or in government.

Though not in good health, in late 2011 he asked Val to drive him to the Lords to add his name to those in favour of voting rights for prisoners.

Chair, British Parliamentary Committee for Iran Freedom (1984–2012)

From Maryam Rajavi, president, National Council of Resistance of Iran

The Iranian Resistance has lost a special friend, the people of Britain have lost one of their admirable symbols in defence of freedom and democracy, and the world community has lost a great man.

During the past three decades, despite his heavy responsibilities at the House of Commons and House of Lords, he always actively supported the Iranian Resistance and sought the plight of the residents of Ashraf. This never stopped even during his last days.

Ten years ago he founded the British Parliamentary Committee for Iran Freedom that rapidly gained the support of the majority of members of the House of Commons and over 200 members of the House of Lords.

He led an unprecedented political and legal battle that successfully resulted in de-proscription of the Iranian Resistance in the UK. He courageously and indiscreetly led a campaign against the policy of appeasement towards the mullahs' regime by British governments, either Labour or Conservative.

Having a profound understanding of the character of the Iranian regime, with an exceptional bravery and subtly, during the last decade he exposed agents and unofficial representatives of the Iranian regime's Ministry of Intelligence and Security outside Iran.

From Alejo Vidal-Quadras

On behalf of my colleagues in the International Committee In Search of Justice (ISJ) and Friends of a Free Iran intergroup in the European Parliament, I would like to express our condolences to Lord Corbett's wife Val and his children, to Mrs Maryam Rajavi and to millions of Iranians inside and outside Iran, who are now mourning the loss of one of their most noble and beloved friends.

I was very much fond of him and the last time we spoke was in June 2011 during a huge gathering of Iranians in Paris, sitting together speaking extensively about our common goals for a free Iran.

Larger than life, he was a great human being, a giant in his own ranks, a man of total dedication to his beliefs, and a tireless campaigner for human rights, especially for the rights of Ashraf residents whom he called the 'bravest of the brave'. He put up a major and effective fight to expose the massive disinformation campaign of the Iranian secret services in Europe against the Iranian Resistance. And he was a pioneer in the de-listing of the resistance in the UK and the European Union, lending his entire credibility, prestige and resources to this cause. His mere presence during the court hearings in the UK went a long way in convincing the judges that the Iranian Resistance was not a terrorist organization. Similarly, he ceaselessly fought against and exposed the appeasement policy of his own government and often openly clashed with Foreign Office officials over this. In a message on his passing, Mrs Rajavi's words were quite apt: 'Lord Corbett embodied the love of humanity and love of freedom, and rebelled against the world of despair and appeasement. He ceaselessly displayed a restive conscience against injustice and despotism.' May he rest in peace.

From a plaque sent to him

Lord Corbett of Castle Vale: A man of honour, who rose to defend the Iranian people's resistance for freedom and democracy amid the reign of religious fascism in Iran. Your courageous defence of the combatants of freedom in Ashraf City will be recorded in the annals of Iranian history for years to come. Maryam Rajavi

Very many tributes were received from Iranians; these represent what most of them expressed.

Robin was one of the most compassionate and courageous men I have ever known. He stood tall, shoulder to shoulder with the Iranian

Resistance against cruelty in Iran. Your loss is my loss. I lost my husband as a result of atrocities in Iran and can imagine what you are going through. I pray to God to give you and your beautiful daughter strength to cope with this loss. One day, the name of Lord Robin Corbett will be the name of many streets, crossroads and squares of cities all over Iran. Robin's name and memory will stay alive in Persian history forever.

Totally devastated to hear about the great loss of Lord Robin Corbett, a true friend to the Iranian Resistance and the Iranian people throughout their darkest days. I lost my brother, a wonderful musician who died under torture. After his sad death, Robin like a true father comforted me. He was like a father for every victim of the mullahs' regime. He was the source of support and comfort, as well as a brave fighter for democracy and human rights in Iran. I feel honoured to have spent time in his presence; may he rest in peace and may his vision of a free Iran be realized very soon. Our history will always remember this great human being who devoted himself to the cause of our resistance against the current dictatorial regime.

Fierce supporter of the Dirty Blood Campaign (1985–2012)

From Sue Threakall, chair, taintedblood.info

In the summer of 1985 I went to see my MP, Robin Corbett. I was outraged and shaken that my husband, Bob, a severe haemophiliac, had been diagnosed with HIV, contracted through his NHS treatment – a blood product called Factor VIII. I didn't know then that Bob was almost certainly walking around with Hepatitis C, plus a myriad of other contaminants as a direct result of his treatment. Little did I know that the meeting with Robin would prove to be such a milestone, and the beginning of a friendship lasting until he died.

Robin took our case very seriously, as he did with all his work with his Birmingham Erdington constituents. We met again at his surgery, he visited us both at home, and we soon learned that he was a big man – not only in stature but also in generosity of spirit and time, in his willingness to go that extra mile, and in his old fashioned gentlemanly manners. He asked questions, and he wrote letters. He persisted, both within Parliament and without, and he never gave up. In fact, a couple of years ago I reminded him of a promise he made to me at the time – that he would stick with this issue until we had achieved justice. We laughed together as I gently teased him, saying that I bet he didn't realise it would go on for quite so long!

I don't think I am pushing my luck if I say that Robin became my friend. He was a friend in high places, yes; but a friend nonetheless. In fact he only mentioned that he had become a lord when one of my letters to him 'went astray', and dismissed it as an almost inconsequential matter! However, in the Lords, as in the 'other place', he continued his support, both of me and of what had now grown into a national campaign. He joined forces with the late lords Morris and Archer, and with Lord Rooker. Together they were formidable. They worked like a small army to support the last government review into contaminated blood, which, though not a conclusion to the campaign, was nonetheless a huge milestone in its progress.

The loss of Robin to the contaminated blood campaign is huge. The loss of this great man to his family and to his friends is all the greater. However, as the years go by I am certain that his legacy will give him a well established and richly deserved place in the history of our nation and in our hearts. Goodbye, my friend, and thank you.

The Castle Vale Story (1983–2012)

From Steve Clayton, Housing and Neighbourhoods Director, Castle Vale Community Housing Association

> 'If there was a Castle Vale stick of rock, it would surely have the word 'Robin' running through it.'

Castle Vale is an outer north Birmingham estate. It was built in the '60s, the largest post-war housing estate in the Midlands with a mixture of 34 tower blocks, houses and maisonettes and home to over 10,000 people.

Unfortunately by the '70s the seeds of decline had already started to be sown: rising unemployment due to the drop in manufacturing, difficult and challenging families moving onto the estate, high crime levels and anti-social behaviour – all resulting in Castle Vale no longer being an area of desire, but a sink estate where people ended up rather than chose to live.

The government at the time established a Housing Action Trust for Castle Vale and over the next 12 years the neighbourhood was transformed, with 32 tower blocks and 2,300 homes demolished, whilst 1,500 new homes were built and over 1,300 improved.

Richard Temple Cox, chief executive of the Housing Action Trust, Angus Kennedy the MD, and Robin, made a formidable team with the vision and fortitude to ensure that any barriers and obstacles met along the way were overcome. Robin was so proud of the achievements of residents in Castle Vale that he chose to include Castle Vale in his title. Everyone was delighted with this and realised that through Robin's activities the name Castle Vale would be recognised both nationally and internationally.

Today, the levels of resident satisfaction in Castle Vale as a place to live are amongst the highest in Birmingham and considerably higher than many of its more 'leafy' neighbouring communities. It is now a place where people choose to live.

How was this transformation achieved? Yes, there was money spent, but strong leadership, vision and unfaltering commitment were all essential ingredients. Robin's boundless energy, enthusiasm and unwavering support for Castle Vale was the 'magic ingredient' that made the difference. He had the rare skill of being able to relate to residents, CEOs, elected members and others, in helping broker ways forward that met the needs of all parties.

As a constituency MP there was none better. Much of Robin's good work was under the radar; there are a countless number of constituents' stories in which Robin has supported them and championed their cause, ensuring the best possible outcome. We heard only a few at the Castle Vale memorial to him.

Robin was chairman of the Castle Vale Neighbourhood Partnership Board (which replaced the Housing Action Trust) until his death. His legacy is that Castle Vale is in high demand with a waiting list of families who want to live there, crime has fallen further and education attainment has improved. Thank you, Robin.

***

When I was about nine years old, my mom, dad, sister and I were living in a two-bedroom three-storey flat on Castle Vale; it was a very nice home but it wasn't big enough. My sister and I were sharing a bedroom (which isn't always great), Star Wars figures and My Little Pony dolls, and didn't get on too well.

Anyhow, my mom was getting no help from the council, so one day she told me we were going to see someone very important, who could help us, and I had to be on my best behaviour. I remember sitting outside the children's room at Castle Vale Residents Association Club waiting to meet this really important person. When it was finally our turn, we went in and sitting behind an old pub table was this huge man with an even huger smile on his face. I remember him being very kind and understanding to my mom but what stands out the most is how he was with me.

Now I was worried about meeting this 'really important' man, but he spent about five minutes asking me about my collection of Star Wars figures that I religiously carried around in a plastic bag. I recall getting them out on the table and telling him about each character and not once did Robin look uninterested or bored with my blabbering about Darth Vader or Ben Kenobi.

I think this shows Robin's impact on those he came into contact with.

My wife Sylvia and I organised a campaign letter with over 200 signatures asking our MP's support to turn Castle Vale around. Robin never let us down. He promised to be at our house for a residents' meeting at a certain time and he was there well before that. Robin took over from there well before the Housing Action Trust came into being. He worked on a number of proposals including the priority of getting a police station on the estate and as many police officers as could be afforded. Which he did. The estate got its first police station and its own dedicated officers. And he and Lady Corbett came to our 50th wedding anniversary celebrations.

His relentless drive and unique ability to work with and rally the residents in order to realise our aims brought success to the Vale. Thank you Robin for your enormous contribution, your achievements and the success of your work in Castle Vale. We will remember you always.

What people said about Robin

Quotes from some of the 900 cards, emails and letters received from former prime ministers, parliamentarians, fellow campaigners and from people he helped.

Over the years in politics and especially in Labour politics, I have recognised that some people have a brilliant talent for the things they care about. And a few have a wonderful ability to tell us about those issues in a way which is clear and compelling. It is a wonderful ability and it has made me care about those same things in a more knowledgeable way. In fact, it has sometimes been a change in my thinking that I didn't anticipate – my understanding has been transformed. Not many people could show me just how wrong the FCO could be and get me to say so in public.

Well, my friend, you have done that for me, and more than once. It is a rare person who can marry together passion and thought and the practical politics, and you are a rare person. I do mean rare. Few can do it with the sincerity and selflessness you so obviously have.

So … apart from everything else I should say, I want to thank you very profoundly.

You are an amazing man and without using a hackneyed phrase other than sincerely, it is an honour to know you.

Robin gave solid service to his constituents; no task was too small to follow up and no issue too small to articulate. He had a very hands-on way of working. If someone came to him, he dealt with the issue himself. His abiding legacy will of course be the Castle Vale regeneration project from which he took his title.

He also had a great sense of fun. He was expert at the supreme party trick. Those who have seen the play 'Jeffrey Bernard is Unwell' will understand when I say Robin called for a box of eggs, a matchbox, a tin lid, one man's shoe and a pint of water. I first watched him perform this in the grounds of Hillsborough Castle in Belfast. He enthralled the audience who all wanted to have a go. Magic. The chair of the Labour peers will be much missed.

Robin was such a vibrant character with a passion for justice, regardless of the popularity or otherwise of the cause. He was never too busy to champion individual constituency cases and was one of the most dedicated and assiduous members of Parliament I have ever known.

I don't cry very often but at least three of the times when I have involved Robin. As an American intern working with him during the 1979 election, I cried when he lost.

Then in 2010 on a trip to London, I felt overwhelmed by emotion as we left the Houses of Parliament after having lunch with Robin, because of his generosity and warmth, his care and concern, and the way he seemed to just pick things up again after 30 years. And, of course, I cried this morning to read the news that he had died.

Your reference at the funeral to him singing after a few glasses of wine brought another round of tears – of joy in remembrance this time. But I think my favourite line is: 'He saw the dog eating the man's dinner.' It has just the perfect ring and tone of one of Robin's hilarious stories. And the whole occasion sounds as if it unfolded exactly how Robin would have wanted it to. I will never forget him.

When I think of him I can't help but think of the link between you – a link that I had the privilege to witness the several times I was with the both of you.

There are couples. And then there's that kind of link between two people – rare in its total trust and openness. I now know it's possible, and that is an inspiration.

For me, even more than Robin's accomplishments – and yours –

that link is what I will remember most. And I know that although the nature of that link has changed, nothing could possibly break it.

That was the most wonderful send-off for Robin. Everyone played their part so well. Your personal tribute was very special, and admirably delivered (and delightful words on the back of the service sheet too). Bruce's professional tribute was thoughtful and pitched just right; Leslie Griffiths gave us sensible spiritual reasoning; Jenny Hill conducted the service with great sensitivity; and the musical interludes allowed us to conjure up our own memories of Robin – fun, and certainly a wonderful personality (but not a saint!). Afterwards we quaffed champagne and some delicious finger food at *The Marchmont Arms*. A wake in the best Irish tradition. We mourned but we laughed as we remembered a great man.

My husband and I have sat and read the tributes to Robin. We shed tears and can only say how much we recognised that dear man. We enjoyed sharing an office with him. He was larger than life and always in good spirits. We so enjoyed our evenings with you both and will cherish memories of the handsome, happy man who was, and always will be, your husband.

I have tears and my throat is choking from reading your speech and all the lovely things people said and wrote. I know how proud you are of Robin's achievement and I know the devotion and the support you gave him during your 45 years of marriage.

It sounds very strange to be writing to you to say how much I enjoyed Robin's funeral. I am sure much as everyone else, I arrived feeling very sad to be saying goodbye to someone I first met 43 years ago. I left feeling lighter and that I had been privileged to have known Robin. I have so often heard the words that we are 'attending the celebration of someone's life', but I have never before felt that was so, and they seemed trite words. On Friday I truly felt that that was exactly what I was doing and we were really celebrating all that Robin had been and done in his life. He achieved so much, but never lost his essential kindness and concern for people. That came through so clearly in the tributes. Also, the happy, fun person that was Robin was not lost. As you said, he was 'not a saint', but thank God for that ... no one loves a saint, and it is obvious so many people loved Robin. You were amazing and I am in total awe of your ability to have got everything so right. He will have loved it.

So many people knew Robin so well over very many years. I only knew him from the times he would come into the House of Lords – and would often berate the nasty Liberal Democrats who sat opposite – and yet we became good friends. His membership on the select sub-committee I chaired was eventful and sparky – all the more so because he had held a much more influential role 'in the other place' – but he generously gave of his vast experience and when he saw me floundering (as I often did) he rode to my rescue.

When later he came onto the board of the Industry and Parliament Trust he became a firm favourite of the staff – and the other trust members who recognised his great knowledge and expertise. How much we could have achieved had he been able to stay with us longer.

This, however, wasn't to be, and all I really want to say, Val, is that he will be deeply missed, in so many ways and by so many people in all walks of life. Your tribute to him made that abundantly clear. He will always live in our hearts and memories.

Robin was a good man and a thoroughly decent individual with a strong social conscience. We remember with appreciation the support of both you and Robin for our club's work in the community, and we know that he was proud to have been elected one of Birchfield Harriers' honorary vice presidents. Robin was a witty and entertaining companion who will be greatly missed by his wide circle of friends and acquaintances.

He was a great soup-maker and I have never quite been able to equal his carrot and orange concoction. But when it comes to cooking, Robin's creamed (definitely not mashed) potatoes were his masterpiece. Christmas wasn't Christmas without Robin singing, but what I loved best was not the actual performance but the numerous false starts as his voice had to be fully prepared and irrigated with vats of white wine.

Robin achieved great things in his life, marrying Val being one of the best, but it is the small things, especially the fun things, that enriched all of our lives that I remember most. How lucky we all are to have known him for so long. We have lost a giant. The kindest man we have ever known.

During our holiday in Oz we went to Fremantle, where Robin was born – a lovely place. Then, the other day, while in a wildlife sanctuary, 'The Wild Colonial Boy' was playing. Fewer verses than Robin always sang but not quite so out of tune. I can remember him on the beach in Cornwall, practising his speech for the selection committee for Erdington. Yelling the words into the waves – whatever; it worked!

We feel fortunate to have spent time with you both and witnessed a partnership of equals up close. We hope it's not too forward to tell you that we've often spoken of how we hope to nurture a similar lifelong connection built upon shared passions and values, a sense of adventure and insatiable curiosity about new ideas and new experiences. Above all we admired your easy playfulness with each other which conveyed a deep love that always managed to draw people closer and closer in.

I did two weeks' work experience with you when I was 15. I can honestly say that after working in your office, sitting in on your advice bureau and actually going on some visits to constituents with you, that every praise given to you is certainly well deserved. I also want to thank you for helping to inspire my interest in politics. Last summer I went to Japan as a UK Youth G8 delegate and am now at university. I take an elective in politics which will make up a third of my degree. Robin's personality filled every room he occupied. How can I ever forget those long Sunday lunches when Robin would demand 'more spuds' to quench his insatiable appetite for potatoes? I don't recall any other Sunday gatherings that were so enriched by the character of just one individual. In addition to good food and wine there was of course plenty of informed and lively conversation – all finished off with the obligatory singing. Thank you for easing us into our new life here in Britain. You all made us feel so welcome and part of the extended Corbett family.

We are still devastated at the death of dear Robin but he has left behind lovely memories. I will always be thinking of him when I smash the crusts of toast and when I mash potatoes. He was the Potato King. And he will always be the 'Wild Colonial Boy'.

Robin was such a generous, funny and humane person. I will not forget how he helped us at a very stressful time in our lives; more than that, he never made us feel as though he was doing us a favour. In fact, quite the opposite. He was so welcoming and friendly from the first minute we met that we took him to our hearts. We always felt secure knowing there was someone to fall back on – a trusted and honest friend. Our children to this day remember the magic shows he did at their birthday parties. May God bless his soul.

Val, a big thank you for looking after Robin so well for so long. He was undoubtedly a star in many ways and he was a natural here at Westminster. He never spared himself and he will be impossible to replace. He led from the front and never failed his colleagues. We share your loss, though you have to bear the greatest burden.

What a heart-warming celebration of Robin's life you shared with those who attended his funeral. What might have been an occasion for much sobbing became a rejoicing for a man much loved who lived life well and for those whose life he had touched. We loved your choice of hymns and music and I heard some singing 'The Red Flag' as his coffin was carried out. The inclusion of Dylan Thomas poetry and the prayer at the end of 'Under Milk Wood', read so well, was brilliant. Robin's spirit will be with you upholding you in whatever you do.

I became very fond of Robin when we worked together as chair and vice chair of the Labour Peers' Group. I shall miss his humour and purpose and kindness.

I have wonderful memories of the BLOODY MAN! It's hard for us to imagine your life without him. You and Robin shared the most beautiful marriage and you shared a special journey together over 45 years, and that is something no one can take away.

I have known Robin for most of my life as a GP, when he was MP for Erdington. During very difficult social and political times the poor and less privileged were well served by his dedication to his public role, his forthright honesty, his ability to listen to the plight of others, and his steadfast determination to follow problems through without being swayed. To then begin to know him socially and to meet you through that development has been a time neither Kate nor I would have missed for anything. Between you, your catalytic effect on my painting career, your timely interference in our intended move to Warwick (which would have been a disaster) and your endless hospitality and friendship have been vital to our lives. Robin will be sadly missed by thousands whose lives he has touched and influenced and his death is the passing of a true Peer of the Realm in so many spheres. We all loved the man that was always larger than life in so many ways.

Robin ... the dedicated, genuinely caring, engaging, determined, generous, driven, honest and creative politician. Our friendship goes back probably well over 30 years and has remained constant throughout. I remember one evening we came to a dinner party at your home and when my husband and I left, our jaws literally ached from laughing most of the evening due to the lively conversation, humour and wit led by the two Corbetts ... what an incredible 'double-act'!

Then I remember the day you and I had lunch in a local restaurant for your birthday and Robin sent a large bunch of red roses to the restaurant for you and a beautiful single red rose for me – how thoughtful and gallant!

It is a very special person who can be so serious and dedicated about what they set out to achieve in their work and at the same time have such a tremendous sense of humour and fun. Robin was always such an incredibly generous host, tremendously entertaining, but also gentle and a great listener as well as a great talker – a rare gift. I send a special salute to 'the great man' ... and his wonderful consort! Robin Corbett – a force of nature, with energy and ebullience and warmth, enough for ten of the finest human beings. Memories of Robin are all of cheerful kindness; all of interest and enthusiasm for issues and facts; all of laughter and irony and the building of relationships for the betterment of people and communities; all of optimism and persistence and a refusal to be defeated.

I hope he knew how much he was loved, and how many people will be without that driving, generous person to touch and hold and love. I'm sure he also trusted that Polly and Val and the rest of us, will continue to feel that positive presence.

I have been a mate of Robin for so many years. I supported him to become our MP in Hemel Hempstead from the start. Robin showed the right way to be a good constituency MP, establishing a network of specialists from every section of the community whom he used to bring to a person's home to deal with the subject. Many times I would knock on the door of a house and say, 'Robin Corbett, your MP, has asked me to look into the problem of condensation/roof collapse/bad drains' … what you will. My love and admiration goes out to him.

I'm sure that taking me under his wing as an intern for the semester I spent in London was a blip on Robin's radar (as he's done so much for so many people), but it was a significant six months in my life. Watching the way Robin took such pleasure in his work was really an inspiration for me. It's something that has stuck with me through the years as I've figured out what I wanted my career to look like. You were both so kind to take me in for lunches, to host our family at your home over Easter and to keep an eye on me during my time on the other side of the pond. I feel lucky to have known Robin, and been privy to his humour, kindness and enthusiasm.

I found Robin's pure, undiluted generosity of spirit endearing. He was always prepared to listen and always took the underdog's side. What great attributes to have as an MP.

One of the times you and Val came to stay with us in Falmouth, my husband took you down the High Street and he bought a beautiful new jacket. Problem was the pockets were sewn up so I said that what was needed was a 'plucker' – lots of raucous laughter at that one. I went and got my plucker and unpicked the pocket and Robin asked Val why she did not have one of these essentials in her sewing kit, again to many cheeky remarks. I gave him the plucker as a gift and off we all went for dinner with Val looking lovely in her carefully thought-out outfit, teasing you as she always does. What a great mate you have found in her, Robin.

We were both in the same branch of the NUJ when we were junior reporters on local papers and the world was our oyster. And here we are, 70 or so years later and still proud to be stalwarts of that particular union.

We have had a lot of fun together over those years and I think that is probably because we have a very similar sense of humour. This was particularly evident in those regular gatherings I organised of the First Day Cover club which you rarely missed. I usually sat you where I could catch your eye, safe in the knowledge that you would send me up and that would get an early laugh.

Many of us watched you together and marvelled at – and maybe slightly envied – your wonderfully close and supportive relationship. Please know that you too, Val, are much loved and surrounded by people who care for you. We will all be here in the months to come.

Robin Corbett was a good and principled man who will be greatly missed in Westminster. As an MP he always championed those causes close to his heart with passion and dedication – whether it be prison reform, animal welfare or safeguarding civil liberties. It was also thanks to Robin that the anonymity of rape victims found its way onto the statute book. Robin was a popular chair of the Labour Peers' Group and I know his colleagues in the House of Lords will miss his wit, passion and good humour. Above all, he was Labour through and through, deeply rooted in values of equality and social justice. Robin was also as loyal and dedicated as they come.

He was such a lovely lovely man – always laughing, jovial and so much fun. He did so much good in his life and was loved by everyone who met him. I think I can honestly say he didn't have an enemy in the world. My niece and nephew still remember our tour of the House of Lords. Robin was the best guide ever and he made every painting come to life.

We will miss Robin so much. We will miss his great laugh and his exuberance and his immense generosity and love of life. I will always remember his kindness to me in our political life in Birmingham – I knew that I could always rely on Robin, in good times and bad, to be supportive, and that is a rare and wonderful thing in politics.

Robin was truly a great man, loved, and a legend in Erdington. He leaves a remarkable legacy of achievement, and it was typical of him that, after outstanding service to the people of Erdington, he went to the House of Lords as Lord Corbett of Castle Vale. He never lost touch with the people he served so well.

Robin was not only a brilliant MP in both Commons and Lords but was a champion of great causes, and underlying his dedication was a deep and long-held commitment to the values of social justice and equality. Its worth is enshrined in the legislation he achieved and in the influence he had on so many he leaves behind.

Robin was a unique human being. He could light up the room with his smile and laughter. He was such good fun. He was a very sincere person, who would always go out of his way to help. I used to say that Robin Corbett would go to London on his hands and knees for a loaf of bread if one of his constituents requested it. He was one of nature's gentlemen.

A wonderful life and a good death, surrounded by family – who could want for more? Robin will be remembered by all of us in the Lords as a marvellous person, full of good humour and with wry intellect.

Robin was a wonderful colleague and an outstanding parliamentarian. I well remember his first entry into the Lords. He could silence the

House when he asked a question, because he spoke with such passion and authority.

Robin stands out to me as an exemplar of commitment to human need in the UK and beyond – he acted as an advocate to people who have no voice and combined toughness as a parliamentarian with gentleness to individuals. On a personal level, his good humour, generosity and the warmth of his affection always left me feeling enriched. I can still picture, vividly, him and Val wearing plastic coronets and greeting me and friends on the doorstep of their Birmingham house just after Robin had been ennobled. He could hardly speak for laughing. A riotous evening followed. I truly thank God for Robin and the impact he had on us and the rest of the world.

Robin was a star, a good colleague and friend who reached out to help. I know, I was on the receiving end of it, for which I will always be grateful and treasure.

You will have received many tributes to Robin's professional warmth and excellence, but I want you to know that on many occasions Robin had cause to help me sensitively and humanly and with great delicacy and love.

Robin showed you could make a difference whilst being a thoroughly decent and principled person.

So many memories of a man I am so glad to have known. He achieved so much for so many people and I have to admit he was always a bit of a hero of mine.

Robin's energy, enthusiasm and zest for life made him many friends, and coupled with his great skill as a raconteur of myriad stories made him a very engaging and valued companion.

His opponents miss him no less than his colleagues.

Robin made me feel very welcome when I arrived in the Lords. Not all colleagues have that natural warmth, and as a newcomer to the House and its many funny ways, I was most appreciative of Robin's support. We had all been hoping that he would soon be back among us, guiding us with his principled approach and easy manner. He is very sorely missed.

He was such a lovely man, with such a warm, kind way about him. Many people who knew him far better than I did will be getting in touch I am sure. I was just the minute taker – but I couldn't have worked for a more benign, unfailingly courteous chair. It was a privilege to work with him and I shall find it hard to believe that at the next meeting we will not hear his voice in the corridor any minute, or see him burst into the room to take his place in the chair with his usual energy. I shall miss him greatly.

Robin was so special. He did so much good. His enthusiasm, vitality, interest in everything, drive, kindness and compassion have changed people's lives, and always for the better. I am in awe of everything he achieved. He made every second count, and the world is definitely a better place because of him. He met hundreds of people every week, yet he always made me feel that I mattered. I can't imagine not seeing him again. He was such an inspiration and I will never forget him. Whenever I think of him, I will smile.

I watched and learned from his statesman-like approach when dealing with opinions different from his own. I admired his ability to rise above party political considerations for the benefit of his community – something I had rarely seen in my local government experience. I also marvelled at his commitment to continue to make a difference long after he finished his term as an MP.

He was always a titanic figure and a man true to his word. We feel honoured to have known him and to have witnessed his iconic leadership and genuine friendship.

He was the man who made it possible for me to sit at this desk right now and email you from the position I am in. His guidance and support have opened doors I never knew existed; I have so much to thank him for.

In addition to the many things that Lord Corbett will be remembered for, I shall always personally remember that he took the trouble to walk us all to the taxis following a dinner in the Houses of Parliament – a mark of graciousness that struck me at the time, and which I hold as an example to many.

Robin was affable, engaging and the antithesis of pomposity. He was a good friend and, as we say in mid-Wales in measured praise, 'a tidy guy'.

Robin always had time for people and making things happen, and I shall always remember his kindness and example of trying to make the world – especially Castle Vale – a better place to live.

I am writing on behalf of the children of Castle Vale, as they do not know how much they owe him. The services, schools and Children's

TOPCLIFFE J. & I. SCHOOL

Hawkinge Drive, Castle Vale, Birmingham. B35 6BS
Telephone: 0121-747 6296 Facsimile: 0121-749 4268

Head teacher: Lauren Gibbons P.D.C.S., A.C.P.

TOPCLIFFE SCHOOL

COMMITTED CARING

Robin at a school with crown painted on his head

66

Centre on the estate provide so much to improve their life chances, and such a lot of this is due to Robin's determination to raise aspirations and his dedication to a just society.

Everyone who met Robin will have felt privileged to have known such a courageous, conscientious friend and hardworking member of Parliament. He had an instinctive feel for what was right, moral and fair.

Having known Robin for almost 30 years, I was always struck by his rare ability to combine idealism with practical politics. A man of principle who had mastered the art of the possible.

One day that stands out to me as an instance of his special qualities was a walk through Birmingham city centre to buy sandwiches for lunch. At one level it was a textbook example of meeting and greeting people; on another it demonstrated why he was such an effective constituency representative. More than once we were halted so he could be thanked for an act on behalf of a constituent, all of which he received with grace, humour and humility. Robin reflected all that was good and generous about British politics, and the Labour party above all. We can ill afford his loss, but his life and work will remain as a shining example for others to follow.

A chairman is a key figure in a clerk's working life and over a career in the House there are few who stand out as genuinely a pleasure to work for. I shall treasure memories of Robin, but carry on regaling my colleagues with anecdotes about him.

Robin's complete lack of self-importance and pomposity, and his warmth and humour, made it a pleasure to work with him. His deep respect for those doing prison reform work was for them a source of strength and reinforcement in what is a difficult and unpopular area.

He was always supportive, generous, good humoured and such a vital presence in any room (or Chamber).

Robin was such a steady, calming influence in politics – heart and head in the right place. I remember well the support he gave to me, and the good, wise advice. I was lucky to have had Robin as a colleague.

He was a great colleague and comrade, always fighting his corner for the causes he deeply believed in. He was one of the few who was a great House of Commons man who became a great and respected House of Lords character. Being the chair of that Labour Lords Group with all its personalities and egos was never the doddle he made it seem – and he did it with such a sense of humour and friendship.

Even when faced with illness he turned up and supported his party and working people; he never complained but carried on doing what he thought was best. It was that spirit and determination that I will remember him for.

His reputation in Parliament is an outstanding example of what the rest of us should try to achieve. He always seemed to me to lead from the front – in terms of his grasp of the subject and innate understanding of human nature. I just wanted you to know how highly Robin was regarded and how much his memory and example will be cherished.

Robin was one of those few people you rarely come across, that when you meet them you realise how very ordinary you are in comparison.

My life has been truly richer for having met Robin.

I'll always remember Robin for his big, beaming smile. His laughter was infectious. Robin made a difference. His legacy will live on in thousands of small acts of kindness he did for his friends, constituents and colleagues.

Robin was an exceptional man. His leadership and commitment was typical of his powerful personality, his courage, his bravery, his sense of honour and respect for humanity.

When he had been elevated to the Lords, and you invited us to stay with you in Birmingham, we have wonderful memories of Robin with arms out-flung, celebrating 'his' Birmingham, as we walked round the city. I seem to remember him embracing a rather astonished bride on our tour as well.

I wanted to say how much I have admired Robin since we first met. As always, I only wish I had written to him to say so earlier on. Perhaps he realised and understood that without my putting it in words. I hope so.

Robin was such fun. He was so positive about people and life. He had friends in politics everywhere. No one spoke ill of him. He was a big personality, full of energy and enthusiasm.

I liked him enormously. He was a determined and passionate parliamentarian, devoted to what was right and fair. Above all, Robin was a much-loved human being who will be missed sorely.

One of his legacies ...

The
ROBIN
CORBETT
AWARD

*All men die but some men live on" -
the quote that inspired the Award*

The background

The Robin Corbett Award for Prisoner Re-Integration was established by members of Lord Corbett's family because he was the respected former Chair of the Home Affairs Committee and for 10 years, until his death in 2012, chaired the All Party Parliamentary Penal Affairs Group. The Award was inaugurated at a celebration of Lord Corbett's life at the House of Lords in June 2012 with the first Award presented a year later at the House of Commons.

"Prison isn't full of bad people. It's full of people who've done bad things and most need a chance to change their lives." - *Robin Corbett*

Do you believe in second chances?

asks Lady Corbett

"If you do, you'll agree that once someone has served their prison sentence, a new start should, and must, be possible.

"Many ex-offenders are motivated by making up for what they did wrong and often prove to be reliable, hard-working and reliable employees. It costs us taxpayers £40,000 to keep one person in prison – every year (Eton costs £35,000). So it makes economic sense to give ex-offenders the chance to change.

"That's what the Robin Corbett Award for Re-integration, set up in my husband's memory, is all about. We fund charities who provide re-integration schemes to help ex-offenders by finding them a sustainable job. A better alternative than a prison cell because 60% of those released will re-offend within two years. That figure drops to 19% for those in employment. The Robin Corbett Award has spawned the Corbett Network, a coalition of more than 50 decision-makers of major charities and organisations aiming to persuade more employers to hire people with convictions.

Main sponsor of the Award is the impressive Chrysalis Foundation (www.chrysalisprogramme.com) while the Worshipful Company of Weavers pay the admin charges so 100% of donations go into the prize fund. The annual presentation take place at either the House of Lords or House of Commons. Details of the latest winners are on the website's Award News page. www.robincorbettawards.co.uk

Applications for the Robin Corbett Award come from prison reform organisations who want to raise awareness of their work, highlight good practice, boost the potential for new partnerships and increase a profile for future funding.

First prize is £5,000; the Highly Commended prize is £3,000 and Commended £1,000. All winners receive a superb glass plaque donated by James Timpson whose company does so much to employ ex-offenders, plus a cheque and a book about Robin Corbett.

We encourage unsuccessful applicants to re-apply because it sometimes happens that a winner, unsuccessful the year before, wins the year after. Applications open in September with the closing date in mid-December. The Awards ceremony is usually in February ahead of the meeting of the All-Party Parliamentary Penal Affairs Group.

"Can't encourage you all to apply enough - this Award has been game-changing for Khulisa - it's added real profile and credibility to our work (helping us to unlock other new funding) alongside the unrestricted £5k prize money itself!"

~ Dominique Airey, Chief Executive, Khulisa (RCA Winner 2018)

The Corbett Network
ENGAGE · EMPOWER · EMPLOY

What is the Corbett Network?

This Network is a coalition of more than 50 decision-makers from leading charities, employers and other organisations who have banded together to reduce re-offending rates by:

- supporting people with convictions in custody and the community
- change their lives by improving routes into meaningful employment;
- helping employers across all sectors access a talent pool of 11 million people with convictions in the UK confidently and effectively.

Why was it created?

Lady Corbett created the Robin Corbett Award for Prisoner Re-integration to create a lasting memorial to honour her husband and his exceptional work as Chair of the All-Party Parliamentary Penal Affairs Group for 10 years until his death in 2012.
"A jail sentence shouldn't be about society's revenge but rather a chance to change the direction of a life." Lord Corbett of Castle Vale

Lady Val kept on meeting people in the rehabilitation sector who were working in their own pond. She decided to ask them to work together in a sea and become more effective. Currently there are 53 who said yes, and the collaboration has been very successful. Alasdair Jackson (CEO Recycling Lives) attended a CN meeting thinking it might be the usual talking shop. The day after the meeting he emailed: "Thought you'd like to know that I've had more people get in touch with me after Wednesday's meeting wanting to collaborate and work together than I've ever had in any previous meeting. The network works...." Nine people contacted Alasdair and they have continued to collaborate, helping, learning and sharing knowledge.

At another Corbett Network meeting Lady Val proposed the creation of an annual Award to be presented to an employer who 'goes above and beyond' in providing meaningful opportunities for people with convictions.

There are two Corbett Network Employer Awards, one for a corporate employer, the other for an SME. Each will also receive an impressive glass plaque donated by James Timpson.

Key Statistics:
- There are over 11 million people on the Police National Computer (PNC) recorded as having a criminal record;

- Reoffending costs the UK economy up to £15 billion per year;

- Over 90% of people convicted each year do not receive a custodial sentence but it remains on their record preventing in many cases loss of earnings;

- Only 17% of prison leavers manage to get a job within a year of release;

- People with convictions who find a job on release are up to 9 percentage points less likely to reoffend;

- 11,000 serving prisoners are employed daily working in prison industries – employed by over 300 businesses or government departments;

- 2,200 prisoners per year are currently doing paid work through Release on Temporary Licence (ROTL);

- 75% of employers admit to discriminating against a candidate with a criminal record

- 33% of people in receipt of benefits have a criminal record.

A growing number of employers large and small have recognised the many positive benefits that people with convictions can bring to their business and have managed to navigate any perceived challenges that recruiting people with convictions might represent. Some have open recruitment policies and practices, some have created dedicated programmes or vacancies, some have put in place a range of mentoring/support initiatives so that people with convictions can continue to rebuild their lives while sustaining employment opportunities. Working with charities, employers know if there is a problem they can rely on the charity to help sort it.

Who are the Networkers?
The full list is on www.thecorbettnetwork.com. They include:
The Clink whose restaurant inside HMP Brixton is justifiably renowned
Recycling Lives providing accommodation, training and permanent jobs for ex-offenders
Mitie Foundation - their Dragons Den-type exercise helps offenders become self-employed
Chrysalis Foundation's courses have helped 100's of offenders get their lives back on track
The New Futures Network aims to get employability coaches in prisons
The Timpson Organisation who have been the pace-setter in giving jobs to ex-offenders

Bounce Back, the 'bridge' between prison and full-time employment.

The Shannon Trust trains prisoners who can read to teach prisoners who can't.

Census Group supports rehabilitation of serving offenders through in-custody work.

WE'VE MADE A VIDEO ...

The Corbett Network recently organised a conference in London, in association with Nacro and Dominic Headley Associates, targeting employers to hire people with convictions. It was a success judging by the forest of hands which went up at the end signifying they had been persuaded. Except only in that conference room. Hence the video.

Reviews make us confident it has a similar result to the conference but on a much larger scale. (See the video link on www.thecorbettnetwork.com)

"They need somewhere to live, a job and someone to give a damn." Maggie Walsh, CEO A Fairer Chance and Corbett Networker

The video shows some committed people working with ex-offenders who <u>do</u> give a damn. Despite the bad publicity prisons receive in the media, there are many people in the prison sector doing their best to support and help ex-offenders to get another chance to get back on track.

Who did we send the link to?
The Corbett Network's 53 members; 780 top business women on the mailing list of Lady Val's Professional Women's Network (a donation from each lunch booking goes towards our charity.) Employer organisations such as the Institute of Directors, HR professionals, Business in the Community etc as well as Youtube, Twitter, Linkedin and the 12 judges of the Robin Corbett Award who are well-connected.

Brexit will mean thousands of vacancies so recruiting from a different talent pool is crucial. We are confident our video will persuade those who view it to recruit from a different talent pool and give another chance to people who have served their sentences and are ready to re-join society.

Lady Val's
PROFESSIONAL WOMEN'S NETWORK
CONNECTING • SUPPORTING • INSPIRING

There's a special place in hell for any woman who doesn't help another woman.

About the network...

For women who work not 'ladies who lunch'

Over 14 years, this Network has connected hundreds of business women to help each other with contacts, knowledge and advice. It also has a strong motivational role as guest speakers are selected to energise and inspire. Our after-lunch free workshops have facilitators who get networkers involved and challenged. Our ice breaker – "How can I help you and how can you help me?" does what it says on the tin and many connections are made leading to new business.

LVPWN organises five lunches a year and speakers have included Dame Stella Rimington, first female Director General of MI5; Gina Miller, constitutional fighter; Cherie Blair, founder of her Foundation helping women in third world countries; Tracy Edwards, round-the-world yachtswoman; Sir Michael Palin, Jon Snow, Prue Leith and Vicky Pryce, prison reformer.

The Network has no joining fee; business executives, senior partners, entrepreneurs and business owners are all eligible to attend.

Lunching with a purpose

Over the last decade this Network's charities have funded NEETS (no education, employment or training) to get job experience through the sadly-lamented Hoxton Apprentice training restaurant where Lady Corbett was an active director. Now the Network raises funds for the Robin Corbett Award for Prisoner Re-integration which annually gives funds to three charities who do the most to re-integrate ex-offenders. An off shoot is the Corbett Network linking over 50 decision-makers of rehabilitation projects working together to support and get jobs for people with convictions. All details of upcoming events: www.ladyvalnetwork.biz

Our re-offending rate of nearly 60% within two years is the highest in Western Europe. That figure falls to 19% when they have a job. As we taxpayers pay £40,000 per prisoner per year and there are 85,000 people incarcerated, it makes economic sense to do more re-integration work and less locking up.

"Prison isn't full of bad people; it's full of people who have done bad things and most need another chance." Robin Corbett

A Last Word from Robin

Speaking in 1997 as MP for Birmingham Erdington.

'I'm not ambitious, not in the sense I'd kill to become this, that or the other. I think of myself more willing than ambitious. I've never planned my life at all. There are times when Val wished I left home at 8.17 every morning and put the key in the latch at 5.19 every evening but she'd get very bored with it soon. I know I would.

'Overall it's been a happy life made better with a happy marriage. I mean, you get one or two knocks don't you, awful ones sometimes. But I've been very privileged in a sense – by and large I've always had jobs which I've enjoyed doing and a great bonus and what's better is that I got paid for doing them!'

A Last Word from Val

I heard this saying from the Ryder golf captain about his friend, Seve Ballesteros, and thought it applied as well to my beloved husband:

'All men die but some men live on.'

Photograph by Susannah Corbett, Robin's eldest daughter. I think it shows his humour and humanity.